30 Minutes
... To Get Your Own Way

30 Minutes ... To Get Your Own Way

Patrick Forsyth

KOGAN PAGE

First Indian Edition 2003
Reprinted 2008

Kogan Page India Private Limited
4737/23 Ansari Road,
Daryaganj
New Delhi 110 002

ISBN-10: 81-7554-215-2
ISBN-13: 978-81-7554-215-0

Published by Vinod Vasishtha for Kogan Page India Private Limited, 4737/23 Ansari Road, Daryaganj, New Delhi - 110 002.

Printed and bound at Print Perfect, New Delhi - 110 064.

CONTENTS

The 30 Minutes Series

The Kogan Page 30 Minutes Series has been devised to give your confidence a boost when faced with tackling a new skill or challenge for the first time.

So the next time you're thrown in at the deep end and want to bring your skills up to scratch or pep up your career prospects, turn to the *30 Minutes Series* for help!

Titles available are:

30 Minutes Before A Meeting
30 Minutes Before A Presentation
30 Minutes to Boost Your Communication Skills
30 Minutes to Boost Your Self Esteem
30 Minutes to Brainstorm Great Ideas
30 Minutes to Deal With Difficult People
30 Minutes to Get Your Own Way
30 Minutes to Get Promoted
30 Minutes to Improve Your Networking Skills
30 Minutes to Make the Right Decision
30 Minutes to Manage Your Time Better
30 Minutes to Market Yourself
30 Minutes to Master the Internet
30 Minutes to Motivate Your Staff
30 Minutes to Negotiate a Better Deal
30 Minutes to Plan a Project
30 Minutes to Solve that Problem
30 Minutes to Succeed in Business Writing
30 Minutes to Write a Business Plan
30 Minutes to Write a Marketing Plan
30 Minutes to Write a Report
30 Minutes to Write Sales Letters

Available from all good bookseller.
For further information on the series, please contact:

Kogan Page India Private Limited
2/13, Ansari Road, Daryaganj, New Delhi-110 002
Tel. 23258325, 23279280, 23283121, 23285874, Fax 0091 11 23267224

INTRODUCTION

'I am not arguing with you – I am telling you.'
James Whistler

Consider how viewpoints differ. First, assume you are standing reading this in a bookshop. I want you to buy this book. Why? Because if you, and a sufficient number of other people, do buy it then I will make some money. Go on, buy it. So far I am probably only succeeding in putting you off. I cannot just tell you to buy it, and expect you to do so just to please me. I have to give you a reason. Well, it is not expensive, its length means you will not tie up an inordinate amount of time reading it, it fits in your pocket and the cover is a tasteful colour.

This is not much better. These are reasons to buy of a sort, but they are subsidiary to the larger issue of what the content of the book is and whether it would be useful to you. Nor will simply inventing something work. You might buy it if I promised it would make you rich and famous overnight, and made you believe it. But that is obviously not credible.

Start again. Think about communication for a moment. It can be difficult. The world is full of communications that are unclear: you fit the thingy into the whatsit and . . . (just try it). Or imprecise: go straight on for about a mile . . . (three miles later . . .). Communication can be made impenetrable by jargon (like calling a spade a manual excavation device), and gobbledegook or 'office speak' (over-formalized business language) can make understanding even more difficult. The confusion that can result may be minor, or it may cause major problems. And things get even more complicated when you want to get someone to do something, when you seek to persuade. In most circumstances, and certainly in the work environment, just saying 'do it' is not enough. It can raise backs, hackles or temperatures; or all three.

Persuasion is not about finding a way of forcing someone to do what you want, it is about getting your own way by making someone feel that it is the right course of action for them as well.

Everyone spends a major part of their time communicating, at work, socially and in all the many interactions we have with other people, and much of that communication is also designed to be persuasive.

So, back to the book: given that it is about making communication persuasive, will you buy it? The answer may still be negative. But how about if the book will help you get your own way more certainly, and more often? If it will reduce the friction of communication breakdowns at work; help you be seen as a clear, authoritative communicator; and if you are reminded of how such agreements can help you save time, money, and so on.

But we are getting ahead of ourselves. Persuasion needs to provide reasons for action, and these are now reasons to buy that affect you. You cannot gain all this just by reading a couple of pages in the bookshop. You do have to read it all; but given those reasons, now will you buy it? After all, if I can make you do what I want and buy a copy, maybe I can help you to get others to do what you want. It's worth thinking about.

Patrick Forsyth
Touchstone Training and Consultancy
28 Saltcote Maltings
Heybridge, Maldon
Essex CM9 4QP
Spring 1999

1

FIRST STEPS

If getting your own way is to be possible – or at least more likely – then you need to gain agreement from other people. Doing so is not about blackmail or brute force; we want people to go along with our ideas willingly. This is not easy. This book would be even shorter if there was some straightforward magic formula, a wand that you could simply wave and guarantee agreement with your every idea. Some ideas find easy agreement; in other instances agreement is difficult and sometimes impossible to achieve.

If I tried to persuade you to put your hand in boiling water, no argument is likely to persuade you. Yet if you have read this far then it may well mean that something persuaded you to buy this book. Persuasion may not be easy, but often it is possible. There are principles and approaches that make a message persuasive, and if you deploy these you are more likely to be successful.

These techniques are not complicated in themselves. By and large they are very much common sense and the complexity comes in orchestrating the process in a way which deploys the techniques appropriately into a flowing conversation. The final approach must be acceptable to the other person and present a persuasive case – one that prompts agreement.

The detail matters here. As we will see, small changes to how an argument is put over can make the difference, turning a 'yes' into a 'no', or vice versa.

Inherent difficulties

Recognizing that communication is never easy is the first step to making your communications successful. Before you have any hope of persuading, you must get people's attention and you must make them understand the meaning of what you say. As mentioned in the introduction, communications breakdowns abound. Homes and offices throughout the land are ringing with voices at this very moment saying 'If you meant that why didn't you say so?' 'But you never said that.' And much more of the same. All of us have found ourselves getting angry with someone when what is actually at fault may be the clarity of our own communication.

Why does this happen? There are a number of reasons, and also a number of ways of acting to get over these inherent problems. So, leave what makes a message persuasive on one side for a moment and consider its clarity.

The problem is people do not listen, find it difficult to understand, are reluctant to agree or act and make things more difficult by providing inaccurate or inadequate feedback. Consider these points in turn.

Paying attention

People find it difficult to listen (or to concentrate on reading), certainly for a long time. Long monologues are resented, and something like this book falls into many sections and uses many headings to provide breaks and stop it being seen as difficult to access. In addition, people are selective. They pay attention to what seems to them to be important and may make the wrong assumptions about what are, in fact, the key parts of a message.

The moral: you have to work hard at making sure your message really is taken in.

Understanding

There are a number of natural human reactions that act to dilute understanding. People always make assumptions based on their past experience: 'Sounds a bit like . . . to me.' If you do not take that into account there can be no frame of reference to which your message can link.

Jargon can be a problem. It may provide a convenient shorthand between people in the know, but can confuse others. Further, people are reluctant to say that they do not understand in case this makes them look stupid.

Assumptions are often made before someone even finishes what he or she is saying, as people say to themselves 'I know where this is going.' At that point their mind stops concentrating on listening and spends more effort on planning a response.

Things spoken but not seen may be more easily misunderstood. Thus showing things may be useful, so too is a message that 'paints a picture'.

The moral: expect achieving understanding to need care.

Agreeing

This takes us further towards persuasion. People are often suspicious of those with 'something to sell'. If agreeing to something might leave them open to being shown to be wrong, and thus involves an element of risk, that too can push people away from agreement.

The moral: even a strong case, which logic dictates should be accepted, may be resisted.

Taking action

Taking action may mean someone has to change a habit (perhaps of a lifetime!). Action also gets people considering the risk: 'If I do this and it doesn't work out, what then?', and some people simply find decision-making hard and will sit on the brink forever if they can.

The moral: even when the argument seems to have been accepted and there is no logical reason not to act, recognize that it may take more to prompt that action.

Obtaining feedback

People are not always open in communication. They may hide their feelings, intentionally or for other reasons (eg embarrassment), or what they do offer by way of feedback may be difficult to interpret.

The moral: feedback needs to be teased out, and it must never be forgotten that appearances can be deceptive.

All this begins to explain some of the difficulties that communication regularly produces. The first job is simply to recognize and remember the likely problems. If you expect difficulties in these kinds of ways then that is the first step to getting over them. There is help at hand, however, because other inherent factors about the nature of communication can act to assist in making it successful; again the trick is to know what these things are, and to use them appropriately.

Aids to understanding

The four factors now mentioned (stemming from what psychologists call the 'laws of learning') all provide assistance to the process. They can be described as:

- addressing the individuals' questions;
- making it logical;
- linking to experience;
- repeating.

Addressing individuals' questions: What is people's first response to any message? They ask about its effect on them. They want to know if it will affect them, and if so whether the effects will be positive or negative. This is surely easy enough to understand; it is what we all do ourselves. Knowing this we can include something about any effects within the message, addressing the problem rather than leaving questions floating in the air.

This may often be as simple as the difference between saying to someone 'Do this and productivity will be improved', and saying something like 'Do this and your workload will be easier to cope with, you will have more time to concentrate on priorities and productivity will increase.'

Making it logical: This is no more than choosing to go through things in a logical order (and perhaps explaining what that order is). Information is better retained in the order in which it is taken in. If we have to re-sort it, something may be lost in the process. Consider something like your telephone number. You know it backwards. Well do you? You certainly know it forwards, but if you try to recite it backwards this involves a different thinking process and probably takes a moment longer.

So, give people things in the right order, no sorting is necessary and they can consider and use the information more easily. If your message comes over in random bits it will not be so powerful.

Linking to experience: Whatever anyone says to anyone else is considered in the light of his or her prior experience. Telephone a supplier to check some detail of your account and consider what goes through your mind if he or she says 'I'll need to check with the computer.' Perhaps this creates a vision of instant efficiency and good service or perhaps not. It depends on what prior experiences with computer systems come to mind.

The same kind of response always happens. If you link accurately to people's experience, understanding is easier. If you misjudge what they know already or assume they have experiences that in fact they have not, confusion can result. Specific linking, eg 'This will be like the meeting we had to discuss increasing sales . . .', with someone calling up the image of a constructive two-hour meeting that really got some new ideas on the go, makes what follows that much easier.

Repeating: Any message, especially a complex one, may be better taken in if it is repeated. This does not mean simply repeating the same words again and again. It means that finding acceptable ways to repeat key parts of a message can be useful in reinforcing understanding.

Considering a number of examples makes this clear (and adding an example is itself just a way of introducing repetition). A meeting followed by the issue of minutes of the proceedings is repetition. Something said and demonstrated, or illustrated by a visual aid, is repetition. So is something that summarizes, or is a checking mechanism. You can probably think of more examples, and are conscious of doing this in various ways already. Deploying repetition as an intentional technique can strengthen understanding and avoid avoidable misunderstanding.

The message here is simple, but has a plethora of implications. Communication can be inherently difficult. It works best if we understand what difficulties are most likely to arise, and why, and if we utilize other inherent aspects of the communications process to assist getting our message over accurately and smoothly.

Understanding, and therefore clarity, is the foundation of persuasion. No one is going to agree and take the action you want if he or she does not know, or is not sure, what it is. With that in mind we can move on to approaches and techniques that will specifically help you to get your own way. The degree of complexity explored to date already implies that this does not just happen.

Persuasiveness comes more certainly with some preparation – and it is to this that we turn next.

2

HALF THE BATTLE

Although it was said earlier that there are no magic formulae, it is not exaggerating to suggest that preparation comes close. It need not take long, but it is always necessary – and it can make all the difference to the chances of success. The person who runs rings around others as it were is probably not inherently persuasive; more likely he or she understands how this sort of communication works and 'does his or her homework'.

Essentially, preparation does a number of things. It:

- clarifies the real purpose of what you want to do;
- provides a 'route map' for what you will do;
- helps you plan the 'shape' of the meeting;
- lets you decide the manner in which you will operate;
- allows you to anticipate and be ready for other people's responses;
- sets up your direction of the whole communication.

We will pick up all these points as we proceed. First, let us define preparation a little more. It ranges from a few seconds' thought before you open your mouth, to a few minutes to get your mind straight about something in advance, to a longer session (including perhaps a discussion with someone else) to thrash out exactly how to proceed. It may be helped by making some notes – either a few words on the back of an envelope or something more. Whatever is necessary, the first rule is very simple – do it.

Whatever form your preparation takes, it needs to go through the following four stages.

Setting objectives

This may sound complicated, or smack of over-engineering, but it is only a way of clarifying your thinking. Many exchanges between people founder because one or both of them is not sure exactly what he or she is trying to do. Consider a simple example: you want your boss to increase your pay. Sounds straightforward, but, on examination, it is actually somewhat vague. What exactly is 'pay'? (salary, benefits, annual bonus and what else?), by how much do you want it increased? (an extra day's pay is an increase, so is 10 per cent more or 50 per cent more), when do you want this to happen? (today, in a month's time, next year?). Many details, these and more, remain unspecified.

A much quoted mnemonic says that objectives should be SMART: that is, specific, measurable, achievable, realistic and timed. How this relates to the chosen example illustrates how viewing objectives in this way helps us have a really clear purpose in mind.

Is it specific? Not very – you may need to put a number, or at least a range of numbers to it before it qualifies as a genuine objective in this sense.

Is it measurable? Not really – practically anything qualifies as an increase. If we put a firm figure to it – 10 per cent, say, translated into an actual figure – then it can be measured accurately. Afterwards you will know for sure whether you have obtained it or not.

Is it achievable? Well, that depends on how it is actually defined. If you decide to go for, say, a 50 per cent increase that might definitely not be achievable; you have to pick a figure that relates not only to what you would like, but also to what is likely to be possible.

Is it realistic? This means not 'Can I get this?' (as above) but 'Should I?'. It is influenced by questions such as: How will your request be seen? Is it reasonable? Will it mark you down as a troublemaker, or a mouse? Taking this broader view is also an important part of setting appropriate objectives.

What timing? This too needs to be specific, and in two ways: first, what do you want to achieve at a particular meeting or at the end of next week? And second, when do you want action? – say, next month's salary slip to reflect an increased figure?

This kind of thinking simply acts to formalize what you want to achieve. It is very difficult to decide how exactly to proceed if your intentions are vague. Clearly stated intentions link logically to a well-planned meeting or exchange, one that is more likely to work for you.

Checking the facts

Some degree of research may be useful at this stage. Research might only be a formal word for what may be a little routine checking. Try to persuade people you have never met of something, and research may be the best word. You may need to find out something about them: what they do, who they work for, what and who they know and how they may think about things. This may mean talking to other people. Externally it might mean checking company directories or annual reports to explore something about the organization for which they work. As we will see, a few more facts may be very useful. And assumptions instead of facts can be very dangerous.

Returning to the salary increase example, a series of simple checks – when you last had an increase, what percentage it was, what trends are current in your industry, what national cost of living figures show, etc – may take only a few moments and yet prove disproportionately useful.

Think here about what you definitely need to have at your fingertips, and what you might need. Doing just a little more than the bare minimum thinking and checking in this way may prove a great asset as communication gets underway.

Planning the meeting

Whatever exchange is envisaged, and it may be your contribution to a meeting, a one-to-one discussion across a desk or a brief meeting 'on the stairs', you need to have some idea of how, ideally, you would like it to go. This means thinking about the structure. What will you say first, second and third? How will you state your case? What examples or evidence do you need? How is it likely to be received? And so on.

The fact that you know no meeting will go exactly as you plan – people are unpredictable – should not negate this thinking. The job will be to get things to go as closely as possible to your ideal, and be able to cope with the differences as well as put over your case. The objectives you have set will influence your decisions here. For example, if the salary increase you want is unashamedly high, then more may need to be done to get the boss to listen and take your request seriously, and more evidence may be necessary to support your case.

Backing up what you will say

Though you intend your argument to be powerful, just stating it may not be enough to get what you want agreed. This part of the planning process is concerned with what can support your case and how it can be organized.

Seeing is believing: think how much more difficult it is to refuse a dessert in a restaurant when there is a trolley of them at your elbow. So think about what you might show someone: a picture, a graph, detailed figures, or an 'exhibit' (as when your decision about which new curtains to buy is influenced by the swatch you take home to look at in your own living-room). The range of possibilities here is enormous. You should ask yourself what would be useful, rather than just what happens to be available, as it may be worth some effort to create something to show.

Whatever you decide to incorporate into the making of your case, make sure it is well organized. It can be impressive to produce something right on cue, perhaps from a mass of material, and it can make a greater impression if it is introduced as being specially for the other person: 'I thought this might make it easier for you to imagine . . .'.

Note also that one of the things that may, in more complex situations, add to your case, is another person. Selecting who it should be, and sorting out who will lead, who will do what and organizing so that you work together seamlessly, needs care. Correctly done, two (or more) people operating effectively together adds to the positive nature of the impression given.

With this thinking done, you are ready to communicate. You know:

- precisely what you are aiming at;
- how you intend to go about presenting your case;
- something about the other person – and therefore his or her likely reactions;
- what you will use to exemplify your case;
- what problems may occur and, broadly, how you will deal with them.

It may also be important to think about certain other matters. For example, how long are you likely to have? It is no good planning a really convincing case that takes half an hour to deliver if you realistically will only have half that time. Or where will the meeting take place? Will there be room for you to lay out all the materials you plan to use on the table? Note: if you have to deal with other than face-to-face meetings, remember that other techniques may be involved, for example writing or 'on-your-feet' presentation*, and that this can add an additional dimension to the process that needs some thought.

You can never know, of course, exactly how things will go and your planning must not act as a straitjacket, but allow you to retain an inherent flexibility. But having all

*Two other titles in this series that may be useful are *30 Minutes Before a Presentation* and *30 Minutes To Write a Report*.

this clear in your mind will certainly help. What is more, it adds another important element to the equation, and to your chances of getting your own way – confidence. If you are clear in your own mind about the path ahead, and have to make less of it up as you go along, then what you do will be easier – and more certain.

3

DO UNTO OTHERS

Preparation, reviewed in the last chapter, may not guarantee success, but it will certainly help. So too does the approach described next. The premise is absurdly simple. You are more likely to be persuasive if you approach the process as something that relates as much to what other people want and how they think as to what you want to do yourself. Indeed this perspective must underlie everything you do, so the starting point is to think through how being persuaded looks from the other person's point of view.

There are three aspects to other people's views that need to be considered and then borne in mind: how they feel, what they want and how they go about making a decision to agree to act, or not.

Others' feelings

Most often people recognize very quickly when they are in a situation where someone is trying to persuade them of something. Their instinctive reaction may be to dislike the idea of it: 'I'm not being made to do anything'; however, once they begin to appreciate what is being asked of them, their feelings may be positive or negative, or indeed a mixture of both. Positive reactions are clearly easier to deal with, and can work for us.

In an obvious case – persuading people to do something they will clearly find beneficial – they may start to see it as a good idea almost at once. So, say to colleagues that you want to discuss some changes to their work portfolio that will make their life easier and put them in line for a salary increase, and you will immediately have their interest. This does not mean that they will not be on the look-out in case what is being suggested is not 100 per cent good, but essentially their thinking will tend to be positive. In this case, there may well be no difficult implications for the person doing the persuading, other than to aim to build on the goodwill that is already starting to exist.

But the opposite may, perhaps, more often be the case. A variety of negative feelings may arise, immediately or as you get into making your case, and if so then you need to be sensitive to what is happening and seek to position what you do in light of it.

The following sets out some examples of how people might feel and what they might think. They might feel:

- *insecure*: this sounds complicated, I am not sure I will know how to decide or what view to take;
- *threatened*: things are being taken out of my hands, I should decide this, not be pushed into something by someone else;
- *out of control*: if I make the wrong decision I may be in trouble, any decision involves taking a risk and things could backfire on me;

- *worried*: you are suggesting changes – does that imply I was at fault before? I don't like that implication;
- *exposed*: this discussion is getting awkward, I am being asked to reveal facts or feelings that I would rather not discuss;
- *ignorant*: you are using your greater knowledge to put me on the spot, I don't feel confident in arguing the point though I am not convinced;
- *confused*: I ought to understand, but you are not making things clear – or letting me get any clarification;
- *sceptical*: you make it sound good, but then it is what you want; maybe the case is not as strong as it seems;
- *misunderstood*: I don't believe the case you make takes my point of view into account – it's all right for you but not for me;
- *suspicious*: people with 'something to sell' always exaggerate and are only interested in what they want – I am not going to be caught out by this.

A moment's thought quickly suggests all such feelings are understandable, but if they are overlooked, if you go ahead as if your message should be received with open arms when in fact such reactions exist, you will hit problems. If these thoughts are in people's minds, then they act to cloud the issue and may make it more difficult to see the logic of something you are suggesting. It is not enough to be clear or to present what seems to you an obviously strong case – the other person must see it as something which he or she can willingly go along with.

What others want

What people want may vary enormously, of course. It will relate back to their situation, views, experience and prejudices. It may reflect deep-seated, long-held views or be more topical and transient, or both. Sometimes you know in advance what people want. On other occasions it comes out in the course of conversation, or you need to ferret it out as you go along. It can be complicated – with a number of different 'wants' involved together (some of which may be contradictory) – and thus needs some thought to keep it in mind. But understanding and responding to people's desires is an important part of being persuasive.

A simple example will make what is involved here clearer. Imagine you have to make some sort of formal presentation with colleagues at work. You want to persuade them to set aside sufficient time, in advance, to rehearse the presentation together to make sure it goes well. What might they want? Maybe to:

1. *make sure it goes well*: as you do, but maybe they are more confident of making it go well than you are;
2. *minimize time spent in preparation*: like you again no doubt, but perhaps this blinds them to the need for rehearsal, which they might see as a sledgehammer to crack a nut;
3. *leave preparation to the last minute*: maybe because other tasks have greater short-term urgency, or seem to have;
4. *outshine you on the day*: they might be more intent on scoring personal points with someone, than on making the overall event go well.

These are examples only. Many feelings might be involved depending on the nature of the presentation, how important it is and how they feel about it. One thing is clear however; such wants make a difference to the likelihood of your getting agreement. Even in a simple example like this, the individual viewpoints are clear:

- on point 1, you all want it to go well, but take differing views of what is necessary to make this happen;
- on point 2, in general you want the same thing, but would define the amount of time that constitutes the minimum differently;
- on point 3 you differ;
- on point 4 there are very personal wants that are, to a degree, outside the main objective involved, that of making your presentations work seamlessly together.

There is a need to balance the differing viewpoints if agreement is to be forthcoming. If you are the persuader, you feel your viewpoint is right – or at least the most appropriate option. How do you move them towards it? Clearly doing so involves them adjusting their intentions. You do not have to persuade them to change their views completely. For instance, they may always see it as easier to do whatever preparation is involved at the last minute, but may still agree to set a time when you want or - and compromise may often be involved - end up somewhere between your two views.

How decisions are made

A good definition of selling is the simple statement that *selling is helping people to buy*. Similarly, whatever the commitment is you are looking to secure, the process of obtaining it is best viewed as one that assists people to make a decision, and which, at the same time, encourages them to make it in favour of whatever option you are suggesting. In a purchasing situation the choices involve competition: if you are buying a washing machine, say, then you may find yourself having to decide whether to purchase the Hoover, the Indesit, the Bosch, or whatever (as well as decide where to buy it from and what to pay). In other situations choice is still involved. In the presentation example used earlier, your imagined colleagues will decide between rehearsing or not, rehearsing earlier or later, doing so in a way that helps them or all of you and so on. Doing nothing may seem, in many circumstances, an attractive option and needs as much arguing against as any other.

It follows that, if a decision-making process is inherently involved, you should not fight against it. The intention should be to help it. Persuasive communication is not something you direct at other people. It is something you engage in with them. The difference is crucial, and anything that leads you to see it as a one-way process is likely to end up making the task you seek to accomplish more difficult. So far so good, but how exactly do people make decisions? The answer can be summed up succinctly. People:

- consider the options;
- consider the advantages and disadvantages of each;
- weigh up the overall way in which they compare;
- select what seems to be, on balance, the best course of action to take.

This does not mean finding and selecting an option with no down sides; realistically, this may not be possible. It means assessing things and selecting an acceptable option, one where the pluses outweigh the minuses. The analogy of a balance or weighing scale is a good one to keep in mind. Imagine an old-fashioned scale with a container on each side. One contains a variety of plus signs, the other minuses. The signs are of different sizes because some elements of the argument are more important than others – they weigh more heavily on the scales. Additionally, some signs represent tangible matters. Others are more subjective, just as, in the presentation example above, achieving the right result from it (say, getting agreement to a 10 per cent increase on a budget) is tangible, whereas individuals' desires to increase their status within an organization through the way they are perceived as a presenter is intangible. Intangible some points may be, but they can still be a powerful component of any case.

A final point completes the picture here: some decisions are more important than others and therefore may be seen to warrant more thought. Where a decision is of this sort people may actively want it to be considered. They want to feel that the process of making it has been sensible and thorough (and therefore the decision is more likely to be a good one); and they may want other people (their manager, say) to feel the same. In either case, this feeling may lengthen the process of persuading them.

The thinking involved

This weighing scale analogy is worth keeping in mind. It can act as a practical tool, helping you envisage what is going on during what is intended to be a persuasive conversation. Beyond that it helps structure the process if you also have a clear idea of the sequence of thinking involved in this weighing-up process.

Psychologists have studied the process. One such way used to look at it is to think of people moving through several stages, saying to themselves, as it were:

- I matter most. Whatever you want me to do, I expect you to worry about how I feel about it, respect me and consider my needs.

- What are the merits and implications of the case you make? Tell me what you suggest and why it makes sense (the pluses) and whether it has any snags (the minuses) so that I can weigh it up, bearing in mind that few, if any, propositions are perfect.
- How will it work? Here they additionally want to assess the details not so much about the proposition but about the areas associated with it (eg in the presentation example: 'Does rehearsal mean I have to give you a written note of what I will say?'; a time-consuming chore and thus seen as negative. Conversely, if this is unnecessary, then that fact may go on the plus side of the balance).
- What do I do? In other words what action – exactly – is now necessary? This too forms part of the balance. If something early on in this book persuaded you that it might help you, you may have bought it. In doing so you recognized (and accepted) that you would have to read it and that this would take a little time. The action – reading – is inherent in the proposition and if you were not prepared to take it on, you might have changed your decision.

It is after this thinking is complete that people will feel they have sufficient evidence on which to base a decision. They have the balance in mind, and they can compare it with that of any other options (and remember, some choices are close run with one option only just coming out ahead of others). Then they can decide; and feel they have made a sensible decision on a considered basis.

This thinking process is largely universal. It may happen very quickly and might be almost instantaneous – the snap judgement. Or it may take longer, and that may sometimes indicate days or weeks (or more!) rather than minutes or hours. But it is always in evidence. So there is always merit in setting out your case in a way that sits comfortably alongside it, hence helping the decision-making process.

Before we move on to how to orchestrate the actual communication and make it persuasive, there is one other factor that also needs to be deployed in a way that respects the other person.

Your manner

Your communication style no doubt reflects your personality. Certainly there is no intention here to suggest that you forget or disguise that and adopt some contrived manner in the belief that this will make you more persuasive: it will not.

On the other hand you do need to think about how you come over. Will it help your case to be seen to be knowledgeable, expert, caring, friendly, responsive, adaptable, secure, well organized, efficient, forward thinking, confident, interested (particularly in the other person or the topic of discussion), respectful, consistent, reliable or whatever? (and what do you not want to appear?). Is it important that you display attention to detail, a respect for the other person's time or that you 'look the part' in some way? Many factors might be involved and such a list could doubtless be extended.

The point is that not only are there many such factors that can be listed, but that they are all options. You can elect to come over as, say, confident or expert (to some degree even if you are not!). You can emphasize factors that are important to the other person, indeed you need to anticipate what these will be. If they want to dot every i and cross every t, so be it; you need to become the sort of person who does just that if it will allow you to get your own way in the end.

This is not so contrived, just an exaggerated version of what we do all the time as we communicate with different kinds of people, for example, at opposite ends of the organizational hierarchy. Again a little thought ahead of actually communicating can allow you to pitch things in the right way, so that your manner enhances the chances of getting your own way, rather than negates them.

Two factors are especially important here: *projection* – this word is used to encapsulate your approach, personality, authority, clout and the whole way in which you come over; and *empathy* – the ability to see things from other people's point of view. More than that, it is the ability to *be seen* to see things from other people's point of view.

These act together. Too much projection and you come over as dictatorial and aggressive. Too little empathy and you seem insensitive and uncaring. You need to deploy both, and they go well together. Sufficient empathy softens what might otherwise be seen as too powerful an approach, and makes the net effect acceptable. This may only necessitate a few words being changed, with an unacceptable 'I think you should do this' being replaced by something such as 'Given that you feel timing is so important, you may want to do this.'

At this point, well prepared and with a close eye on how the other person will consider your suggestion, and in what way he or she will go about coming to a decision to go along with it or not, we can turn to how to structure and put over a persuasive case.

4

COMMUNICATING A PERSUASIVE CASE

Your communication may take various forms, but let us consider the ubiquitous meeting. This may be formal, with two (or more) people sitting comfortably around a desk, or happen on the move (walking from the office to the pub for lunch) and sometimes it will occur in more difficult circumstances (a discussion, on your feet, in a factory with noisy machinery clattering in the background). In every case the objective is the same: to create a considered message that acts persuasively to prompt someone to take whatever action you seek.

In order to be able to proceed on a considered basis, you need to draw on a clear view of what is happening during such a meeting. We will dissect the process to tease out the key issues.

First impressions last

The manner you adopt, and the preparation you have done, will both contribute to your making a good start. So too will your attitude at the beginning. You need to take charge. View it as your meeting. Make it one that you will direct. This need not imply an aggressive stance. Just as a good chairperson may not speak first, loudest or longest, you can be in charge without making the other people feel overpowered. So, take the initiative and aim to run the kind of meeting you want, and that the other people will find appropriate or like.

The first task is to get their attention, to make them concentrate on the issue at hand. You will never persuade anybody of anything if they are not concentrating on, and thus appreciating, what is involved. Imagine what they are thinking: is this going to be interesting, useful or a waste of good time?, and aim to make sure that their first reaction is as you would want it. So far so good. Let's see what they have to say.

To create this impression it helps if you:

- appear well organized and prepared;
- suggest and agree an agenda that makes sense to all of you;
- make clear how long the session will last;
- get down to business promptly.

Overall, if in the first moments you show interest in one of the people and make it clear that he or she is important to the proceedings, this will certainly help. Even something as simple as a little flattery may help: 'Some of your good organization would help here, John; can you spare 10 minutes to go through . . .'. Of course, not everyone is taken in by this sort of thing . . . though if you respond to that thought by thinking 'Yes, I'm not that gullible', then you have just demonstrated how well a little flattery works.

Finding out

With the meeting underway, the next stage is to find out something about the other people's perspective on the matter. For example, returning to the example of a presentation rehearsal, it may be useful to know whether your colleagues:

- want to rehearse;
- need to do so;
- see it being done at any particular moment;
- envisage it taking a particular amount of time

and what they believe the presentation should achieve and how it might be done; and so on. Having some knowledge of this kind of thinking, and perhaps of their presentational abilities, shows you something about the job of persuasion to be done. This may range from a major battle (they do not want to do it at all), to a near meeting of minds (you all see the need, but you are going to have to persuade them to give up longer for it than they envisage).

Such finding out is achieved by asking questions – and listening to the answers. Each is worth a comment.

Questioning

What to ask and how to put it may need some thought as you prepare. You need to phrase questions clearly and it is useful to use three levels of questioning:

Closed questions: these prompt rapid 'yes' or 'no' answers, and are useful as a starting point or to gain rapid confirmation of something.

Open questions: these cannot be answered 'yes' or 'no' and typically begin with the words what, why, where, when, who and how and phrases such as 'Tell me about . . .'. They get people talking, they involve them and they like the feeling they give to the conversation.

Probing questions: these are simply a series of linked questions to pursue a point: 'Tell me more about . . .', particularly to get to the why of the matter.

To extend the example: ask your colleagues if there should be a presentation rehearsal and the yes or no answer tells you little. Follow up a yes answer by asking why they think it is necessary (an open question) and you will learn more: 'I'm really a bit nervous about the whole thing', and more questions can then fill in the detail.

It is important here that people appreciate what is happening. Clever questioning may provide you with a useful picture, but this needs to be seen to be the case. You will persuade more certainly if the other person knows that you understand their position.

Listening

It is very easy to fail to listen as carefully as you should. Imagine someone says to you: 'The sky is bright green today, so . . .'. You disagree. Manifestly it is blue. What is your mind doing? Not listening carefully to what comes next, but planning a riposte. Watch for others doing this to you; it is a classic cause of misunderstandings.

The moral is to listen carefully, concentrate on listening, ensure points register or make notes and be sure nothing distracts you. It helps too if you look like a good listener, paying attention to what is being said (good eye contact helps here) so that you seem interested.

Make no mistake, finding out can give you information that becomes the basis of successful persuasion. If your fellow presenters let slip that their boss has said this 'better go well', then later you might use that as part of your argument: 'Given what your boss said about it, perhaps the time we spend beforehand could be a little longer.'

Next, with some information to hand you can begin to put over your case.

The power of persuasion

My dictionary says of the word persuasion: 'To cause [people] to believe or do something by reasoning with them'. Fine, but the question is how to do this. To be persuasive a case must be understandable, attractive and credible. Consider these points in turn.

Creating understanding: a good deal has been said already about the need for clear communication. The point here is more than simply avoiding misunderstandings. People like clarity of explanation and ease of understanding. Spending five minutes digressing, only to have light dawn at the last moment in a way that gets the person thinking 'Why ever didn't you say that to begin with?', hardly builds your credibility.

When people find something they expect to be difficult to understand easy, they like it. A powerful description, especially one that puts things in terms the other person can identify with, can strengthen a case disproportionately. Care is sensible here. Avoid inappropriate use of jargon: it is only useful shorthand when both parties have the same level of understanding of the terminology involved. You only have to think about computers to observe the problem. So, always:

- think about explanations and descriptions, try them out and be sure they work;
- aim to make what you say immediately and easily understood;
- be thorough and precise, telling people enough detail to make the point and emphasizing the most relevant points;
- match the level of technicality you use with the other person (and avoid or explain jargon if it might confuse).

This is an area where you can score some points. Think about the structure and sequence of what you say and how it breaks down into subsections, present a logical and organized case and signal what you aim to do in advance: 'It may be easiest if we go through this in stages. Let's consider the timing first, then the costs, then how we need to organize implementation.' If such a start gets people nodding, then you will carry them with you to the next stage. Use as many layers of this as is necessary to keep things clear, in the example adding: 'Timing implies when we will do things and how long it will take. Let's discuss duration first and then it should be easier to see when things can be fitted in.'

Already what you achieve in this respect can begin to put some convincing pluses on the positive side of your balance.

Making the case attractive: this part of the argument has to set out the core pluses of the case, painting a picture of why agreement should follow. You get your own way when people see what something does for, or means to, them. How this is done is largely a question of giving the argument a focus of what, in sales jargon, is called benefits, rather than features. Benefits are what something does for or means to someone, whereas features are simply factual points about it. The spell checker on my computer is a feature. Being able to produce an accurate manuscript quickly and easily, the time and effort saved and the avoidance of material being returned for correction (by a boss, customer or, in my case, editor) are all benefits. They are things the feature – the spell checker - helps me to do. Features act to produce benefits.

The sequence here is important. Just tell people everything about a suggestion in terms of its features and their response may well be to say (or think) 'So what.' Start by discovering what they want, then show them that what you are suggesting provides that and then the feature may reinforce the argument.

Returning again to the example, saying 'A rehearsal will only take an hour' (the duration is a feature) may have them saying 'How long?' in horror at what they see as a long time. Get them agreeing that the presentation must go well: 'Yes, really it must', and that there is a great deal to gain from it: 'Right', and that there is a possibility of presenters falling over each other's feet unless there is a rehearsal. Then the ability of the rehearsal to increase the chances of success (which is what it will do and is therefore a benefit) makes much better sense.

The principle described here is important. By thinking about the elements of the case in this way and, as you do so, adding to each point the thought 'which means that . . .', you can tease out the most powerful description. This is a short book (short is a feature) which means that: it does not contain many words; it does not take too long to read; you can apply any lessons you learn from it fast; you might be able to get your way about something you have to discuss tomorrow. All this analysis moves the case more and more towards something it will do for you (a benefit). If I was addressing an individual whom I knew wanted to raise the matter of a salary increase tomorrow, then the case could be personalized and the benefit described made specific.

The task therefore is to make a clear case, to emphasize aspects of the case that have a positive effect on the other person and to make sure there are sufficient, and sufficiently powerful, pluses to add up to an agreeable proposition.

But there is a further element to making a persuasive case. It needs to be credible.

Adding credibility: because of the inherent suspicion that tends to exist when selling or persuasion are in evidence, people's reaction to your saying that something is a good course of action to adopt may simply be to say: 'You would say that wouldn't you!' Your say so is not enough. They want more. Credibility is added to your case by offering evidence, other than your opinion, that the case really is sound. The salesperson selling a car who says 'The Automobile Association test results show it does 45 miles per gallon' is putting a reliable source ahead of the figure they want to quote, and boosting the weight it adds to the argument.

Such credibility can be added in many ways, for example:

- quoting past experience: 'The project approach is very like . . .' and that worked well;
- involving the support of others (a person or organization): 'The Training Manager says a rehearsal would be useful' (when the other party respects the person referred to);
- quoting measurement of results: '50 per cent of these types of presentation end without securing agreement, let's make this one of the successful ones';
- mentioning any guarantees, tests or standards that are met;

- invoking quantity that reinforces the case: 'Several departments work this way already, hundreds of people use it.'

It is worth thinking about both the need for proof and how strong that need might be, and thus what evidence can be used in support of your argument before exposing any case to others.

A final point here: remember that people's perspectives on some things may not be solely their own. They might react with their employer or department, their boss, their family, or their staff in mind. Equally, they may react positively for reasons of common good, because their helping you will help make the department you work for more efficient, or very personally, they want to be seen to be involved in something – or you promised them a drink in the pub!

Feedback

At this point – blending your message to ensure it combines being understandable, attractive and convincing – you may feel you are making a powerful case, but it is dangerous to assume so. You need some feedback and it is important to include obtaining it in your approach. It is very easy to find that your confidence in a well-planned argument makes you forge ahead without pause, only to find later that they were with you only up to the moment you said 'Right, let's make a start!'

Feedback can be obtained in two main ways:

1) Observation – look and listen. Do they look interested or are they tapping their fingers impatiently eager to butt in, or gazing out of the window in boredom? Do they sound interested? Watch for remarks such as: 'That's interesting . . . I see . . . fine . . .' and for phrases

that imply agreement: 'OK . . . should work . . . why not?'.

2) Ask questions – to check understanding: 'Is that clear? . . . so far so good?'. To check their appreciation of benefits: 'Do you agree that would simplify things?'. Or to check their reaction to features: 'How does an hour's meeting sound?'. Or to check their perspective: 'You did say it would be best for you before the 10th?'.

Responses of all sorts will clarify the picture as you go, helping you adjust your approach if necessary, and allowing you to focus on those areas that appear to act most readily as foundations of agreement.

Summary

The key approaches involved in making a persuasive case are:

- to be prepared;
- to get off to a good start;
- to ask questions to establish others' needs or interest in the issues;
- to structure your approach around the other person;
- to take one point at a time;
- to proceed in a logical order;
- to talk benefits: tell them what your proposition will do for, or mean to, them;
- to always be clear and descriptive;
- to provide proof to back up your argument if necessary;
- to check progress by obtaining feedback and keeping the conversation two way.

So far so good. If you make a powerful case you might move straight to agreement. Might. More often people have, in part at least, negative responses – they see a balance with some minuses as well as pluses. And maybe they see too many minuses to allow agreement. They object, in principle or to particulars, they confirm the old rule that there is always a but.

5

SECURING AGREEMENT

The better you present your case, and the better it is directed towards the person in question, reflecting his or her situation, needs and views, the less objections you are likely to get. So, although you are almost always going to get some, the first strategy is to reduce them by presenting a case that is 'on target' in this way.

Anticipating objections

The second point to bear in mind is that often it is not difficult to anticipate the nature of objections. If you know your fellow presenters in our example are busy, perhaps with a major project with pressing deadlines, then it should not be surprising if their first response is to find the time a rehearsal will take unacceptable. Anticipation does not mean objections then become easy to deal with, but at least you have time to consider how best to handle them.

That said, sometimes the way in which routine objections arise can be surprising. Something you expect to be a major issue fails to materialize, something minor assumes giant proportions or something comes up late when you expect it early on, or vice versa.

Whatever objections may be about, they need handling. Ignored, unexplained or allowed to retain a major role in the balance, they can push the total balance into the negative – and the result is that you fail to get agreement.

Options for handling

The first thing about objections is to recognize that they are likely to occur and to take a positive view of them. Think of them from others' points of view for a moment. They are trying to assess your proposition – weighing it up – and they think there are snags. They want you to take any point they raise seriously, not to reject it out of hand, which will seem unreasonable.

So consider some initial factors as rules:

- regard objections as a sign of interest (after all, why would anyone bother to raise issues about something they had already decided to reject);
- anticipate and, perhaps, pre-empt them (especially regularly raised issues);
- never allow arguments to develop (especially not of the 'yes it is, no it's not' variety);
- remember that a well-handled objection may strengthen your case.

Thus the first response to an objection being voiced should be not a violent denial, but an acknowledgement. This may only be a few words: 'That's certainly something we need to consider', 'Fair point, let me show you how we get over that', but is an important preliminary. It acts to:

- indicate you believe there is a point to be answered;
- show you are not going to argue unconstructively;
- make it clear your response is likely to be considered and serious;
- give you a moment to think (which you may need!);
- clarify what is really meant (if it is not clear what is being said, or why, a question may be a valuable preliminary to answering).

A well-handled acknowledgement sets up the situation, allowing you to proceed with the other person paying attention and prepared to listen. But you cannot leave things hanging long; you need to move on to an answer. The ways in which negative factors can be handled are mechanically straightforward. There are only four different options, though all of them may need to be used in concert with stressing, or stressing again, things on the plus side of the balance. The four options are:

1. *Remove them*: the first option is to remove the objection, to persuade the people that it is not actually a negative factor. Often objections arise out of sheer confusion, for example: 'I don't have time for a full rehearsal!'. This is based on an overestimate of how long it will take. Tell them that what you have in mind is an hour or so, and not the whole morning as they envisaged, and the objection evaporates.
2. *Reduce them*: or you can act to show that although there is a negative element to the case, it is a minor matter: 'Getting this presentation right is so important, it will take a moment certainly, but surely an hour or so is worthwhile?'

3. *Turn them into a plus*: here you take what seems like a negative factor and show that it is, in fact, the opposite: 'Rehearsal seems elaborate and it will take an hour or so, but we all have to do some individual preparation. Rehearsal will halve that time and ensure the presentation goes well.'
4. *Agree*: the last option, and one that the facts sometimes make necessary, is to agree that an objection raised is a snag: 'You're right, it is time-consuming, but this presentation has to go well and there is no other option.'

Because there are only four options for dealing with the matter, the process is manageable and it should not be difficult to keep it in mind during a conversation and decide, as something is raised, how to proceed.

In every case keep the vision of the whole balance in mind. The job is not to remove every single minus from the negative side (there may well be some snags and this is simply not possible), it is to preserve the overall configuration of the balance you have created in the other person's mind.

Excuses

Let us be honest, sometimes people disguise their reasons for not acting as we wish. They say 'It will take too long', 'The cost is too great', or whatever when they are simply being stubborn. In this case you need to try to recognize what is an excuse and what is not. A long justification of time or cost will achieve nothing if that is only a disguise for the real reason. For example, suppose your fellow presenters said they did not like the thought of presenting with you. Maybe what they are saying is that they are not very confident of their presentational skills and do not want you to witness them.

Suspect something like this is going on and the only way forward is to ask questions, and perhaps to drive things out in the open: 'Be honest, that's not really an issue. Why do you really object?'

Reaching a conclusion

Once your case is explained and all objections have been raised and dealt with, what next? It is easy to leave things without getting a decision. 'Has that given you all the information you need to make a decision?' is polite, but may just prompt someone to agree it has, and try to drop the conversation for the moment.

You have to *ask* for their agreement.

If you have made a good case, this is not so much part of the persuasion; rather it is only aiming to convert interest and agreement into action. You simply need to ask, and there are a variety of ways of doing this, for example:

- just ask ('shall we put a time in our diaries?');
- tell them. You may not have the authority to instruct them, but make it sound like an order ('put something in your diary');
- suggest why it is a good idea to commit now rather than later ('let's set a date now, while we can find a mutually convenient time that does not disrupt anything else too much');
- suggest why it is a bad idea to leave it ('unless we set a date now, we will never find a convenient time');
- suggest alternatives, positive alternatives where agreement to either one gives you your own way ('so, shall

we clear an hour for this or make it two?'). And repeat as necessary ('so, an hour it is then, this week or next?');

- assume agreement and phrase the request accordingly ('fine, we seem to be agreed, let's get our diaries out and schedule a time').

Sometimes, after what has been a long, complex discussion, it may be useful to summarize as you conclude, touching once more on the main advantages of the action to which you seek agreement.

What next?

At this point you may get agreement – or not. We all need to be realistic about this. No one always gets his or her own way – what we want is a good strike rate as it were, and going about it the right way helps achieve this. But there are other considerations. First, you need to deal with indecision. If someone says he or she wants to think about it, always agree: 'OK, it's an important decision, I can see you want to be sure.' But then try to find out why this is necessary: 'But are there any particular things you are not sure about?' Often something will be identified, maybe several areas (try to get a list), in which case assume the conversation will continue, revisit them and then move back to asking for a commitment as if there had been no hitch. Often this will then get a decision.

Second, you must follow up persistently. If things have to conclude on a 'leave it with me' basis, agree the timing, keep the initiative: 'Right, I'll give you a call on Friday and we will try to finalize things then.' Always take the follow-up action as planned, and go on doing it as long as necessary. Take all delays at face value. If a secretary says someone is in a meeting, assume that this is true, and move on: 'When would be a good time to contact them tomorrow?'. Giving up can simply see agreement going by default for no good reason other than your lack of persistence.

Summary

Those most likely to get their own way do not charge at the process like bulls at a gate. They treat people with respect, trying to understand their point of view and use that in the argument. They may be assertive, persistent and thorough, but they are not aggressive (that may work once or twice, but is likely to cause resentment and make things more difficult in the long term).

They go about things in a systematic way, after spending some time preparing, and are patient yet insistent. People may agree to things for all sorts of reasons. For instance, before sending this manuscript to the publisher, I got a colleague of mine to check it for me on a swap basis. He agreed to do that for me in return for something I could do to help him save some time. But what persuades most readily is a reasoned case, something designed to make the particular individual (or individuals) respond positively because it is designed to persuade.

Practice makes perfect and persuasion is as much an art as a science. But, given that, the techniques certainly help, and understanding them is the first step towards drawing on them and deploying them appropriately to help you get your way more often and more certainly.

AFTERWORD

'Most people do not admit that they engage in selling . . . But if you are pursuing power, you are selling almost all the time.'

Thomas Quick

We spend most of our lives, at work and in social interactions, communicating. Most of the time we may think little about it. But we notice quickly enough when something goes wrong. Communication can be inherently difficult. It works more effectively and more certainly when it is thought about, when the message is considered. This is doubly so if there are any special factors involved, and communicating persuasively – setting out to get your own way – is certainly a greater challenge than simpler forms of communication.

In this brief text you will have got a flavour of how to be persuasive, and to present a persuasive case – one that will give someone reasons to give you your own way. There may be no simple formula that guarantees success, but there are a number of principles and techniques that smooth the way and make getting your own way more likely. While you will never win them all, as it were, you should be able to achieve a good strike rate.

At the same time persuasion cannot be deployed 'by rote'. There can be no 'script', and although there are guiding principles, there is no set way of proceeding that allows you simply to follow the rules on 'automatic pilot', each time. The approach you take needs to be tailored, case by case, person by person. Similar thinking may be involved in analysing the situation and deciding on the precise approach, but what works today with one person is just that. Tomorrow, next week, next year, or with someone else, something different may be needed. And the adaptation might involve changing a word or two, or adopting a radically different approach.

This type of communication must be approached in a tailored way, and as circumstances change – who we are aiming to persuade, how they think and what affects them, and so on – the approach needs to accommodate them. Thus we will all spend a lifetime honing our skills, not only to become better at deploying them, but also to better fit them to whatever the current circumstances may demand. Recognizing that this is necessary is the first step towards keeping your skills ahead of the game and maintaining an acceptable success rate.

So, practice makes perfect. You need to bear in mind the guidelines set out here and give them a try. If things do not go perfectly at first – no matter. It is a step in the right direction. The trick is to learn from your experience, to observe and recognize what went well and what went less well, and adapt as time goes by. The maxim about practice is attributed to more than one sportsperson: 'It's a funny thing, but the more I practice, the more my luck seems to improve', but contains a clear truth.

Making success more certain

Of course, as has been made clear, a wealth of detail is involved, but let us conclude with a manageable number of points that, while not negating any others, are important. Overall there are perhaps three. First, you should prepare carefully. So much stems from the thought you put in before you even open your mouth. Preparation is key. Make time for it, make it constructive and everything that follows will be that little bit easier. Second, adopt a consciousness of the whole process: being aware of the processes, approaches and techniques and how they all fit together is the first step to deploying them in a way that makes for effectiveness. The orchestration of all this may seem difficult at first, but the habit of keeping the overview in mind builds up, especially if your aim is that it should, and this quickly begins to make the process easier and more manageable. And finally, be confident. If you have thought through what you intend to do, if it is based on sound principles and you know that this is the case, then you can afford to be confident. There is a virtuous circle here. Being confident shows. The case you make is then judged differently. It may seem more credible if you have the courage of your convictions, and if so, then as it begins to work, positive feedback can raise your confidence still more.

If you recognize that all this is possible, if you see the necessity for a considered approach and go about building your case with care and putting it over with precision, then you may well surprise yourself with just how persuasive you can be. If you intended to become more persuasive, then you have just got your own way – on this at least.